Strategising the Game of Futures & Options

How about you
change the game ?

Your Magic book to Win

Bill Lucre

First Published in **October 2024**

ISBN: 978-93-6356-796-2

PUBLISHING MONGERS

+91 9311101365

Distributed by: Watergies

Preface

A game where you know the codes, where you know you will almost never lose until you are blatantly wrong. A market where taking a risk that leads to a loss is not an option. A market where you make money no matter what. A code to help you win, a code to change the game.

Foreword

The author takes you step by step through multiple strategies that shift the odds in your favour. Nothing is sure short in the market but the author helps you with various strategies that make it easy without uncertainty in the market and even if there is uncertainty, the author tells you how to maximise your profit with it. Trading is never simple, but it becomes much less complicated with these strategies at hand.

Acknowledgments

A heartfelt thanks to the publishing team for everything you have done for me and investors all across the globe.

About the author

Just an investor who learnt it all with experience.

Dedication

This one is for every investor who trades in futures and options and for whom loss in not an acceptable option.

Introduction

Trading futures and options is a zero sum game, someone is always going to lose, but how about you change the game. How about you have a code at hand that will almost never let you lose, a code that rewards you even when you are right, and even when you are not wrong. It requires simple disciple and adhering to this set of strategies. It is time to change the game, it is time to shift the odds in your favour, it the time of Strategising the Game of Futures and Options because losing is still not an option.

Prologue

It is literally free money, why not grab it.

So, you want to dabble in the world of futures and options, how about you stop losing money and start winning for a change.

It requires discipline. Do you have it ?

You cannot blindly go buying and selling options because you have a feeling in the gut that the market is going to rise or fall from here. You might be right, but just not right now and you end up losing money. Always remember there is a fifty percent chance of you losing money either way.

But, what if you change the game ? If it was possible for you to be right in the long run or even be not wrong i.e. the market does not move and you end up earning, a game where time plays for you along with intrinsic value. The only way to achieve it, is to strategise. To understand these strategies, you need to know the concepts from the book 'Playing the Game of Futures & Options' and the odds will always be in your favour.

Once you are through with the concepts of how you need to adapt these strategies, let us go through them one by one.

Call Spread

A combination of buying and
selling calls to achieve the
desired result

Call Spread strategy is a combination of buying and selling your call options of the strike price you predict for the market to attain.

Call spread can be used to achieve either a bullish result or a bearish result.

The risk can be minimal or high depending on what you want to achieve. With time in your favour, you need to achieve your target anytime through the period. The longer you stay in the trade, the more you earn because time is on your side.

Let us see how we can use it for our bullish strategies as well as our bearish strategies.

Bullish Call Spread

In a bullish call spread, you buy a call option at the current strike price and sell another call option below it. It could be one strike below or five strikes below depending on what you want to earn, and how much you want to risk. Now, with just a little movement upwards, you start earning and you can stay here until the expiry to win all you had expected, or if the market moves in your favour, along with time, you keep earning more. Most of all, if the market turns against you for some time, the longer time it spends down there before going upwards, the more you earn. In this strategy, time becomes irrelevant for you if things are not working out. You just have to not be wrong one day until the expiry of your contract for you to exit. Exiting will again depend on you i.e. how much do you want to take home. Some people wish to sit until expiry to take home everything that they can get, no matter the risk. But, you should never tempt fate. If you are in, you are getting something, take it and go home. Come back with a new trade. You can easily lose all you have gained and much more. If you increase the gap of your sell, you risk more and earn more. Similarly, if you sell a call higher up than the spot price, you start earning with the moment it turns in your favour, and on the day of the expiry, you earn even if the market just missed your target. It works wonders after a correction in the market when you are sure for it to rebound to its high, even if it takes some time to get there. With time in your favour, you are almost sure to win.

Bearish Call Spread

A bearish call spread works inversely in comparison to a bullish call spread. Here, you sell a call option at the spot price you hope for the market to not cross, and buy another call option few spots above that. Here again, your maximum loss is capped and so is your maximum profit. Even if the market breaches your prediction for some time before your expiry, you can ride it out. The longer you stay in the trade, the more you earn. You just have to be correct by one point to earn your maximum on the expiry. Time is in your favour and even you are neither right nor wrong, you get rewarded. The choice will again be yours as to how much do you want to take home in the trade. Assuming you just got in the trade, and the market moves in your direction, you are going to make approximately twenty five percent of your gain. Now, you have to decide whether you want to secure that twenty five percent or do you want to wait until expiry to take it all. The market sentiment and the general trend also play a major role in influencing your decision. But, on the other hand, if you have been in a trade long enough and you are still on the border and you still face the risk of a more bullish move before expiry, it is safer to exit, safer to take home a percentage rather than give it away. Time and intrinsic both work for you here. If the market stays just a little in your direction, time helps you, but if intrinsic moves heavily in your direction, time might not even need to help you, but rather intrinsic alone will get you to your maximum gain.

Put Spread

A combination of buying and selling puts to achieve the desired result

A Put Spread is a combination of buying and selling put options for the strike price you predict for the market to breach, attain or hold.

A Put spread strategy can be used either for your bearish trade or bullish trade depending on what you buy and sell.

The risk will always be capped, but you have to decide whether you want a high risk trade or a minimal risk trade. The profit will be directly related to the risk, but time will help you overcome it.

Let us see how we can use the put option strategy for our bullish or bearish trade.

Bullish Put Spread

In a Bullish Put Spread, you sell a put option at the strike price you predict for the market to breach and you buy another put option a few strikes below depending on your risk appetite and the profit you are targeting. The more the difference between the two, the more the profit. In either case, you are hedged and your maximum loss is known to you at the time of entering the trade. If you are trading with this strategy at the current strike price, and the market does not turn out bullish, you still win. If the market takes a turn in your direction, you win immediately. But even if the market goes against you for some time, and then comes back, you still win, and as always, the longer you stay in, the more you win. You just need to be correct or for that matter, not wrong, one day until the expiry. Even if the market crashes, your loss is still capped and there might still be hope of a recovery, so once you are in the trade, and the market becomes unfavourable, you will not keep losing money with every passing moment, but instead you will still have hope of ending this on a win. How long you want to stay in the trade, that is again upto you, you just don't have to be wrong once, at any point of time until expiry.

Bearish Put Spread

Exactly opposite to a Bearish Call spread or a Bullish Put Spread is a Bearish Put Spread. In a bearish put spread, you buy a put option of a strike price you predict the market to not breach, and you sell a put option a few strikes below it. Again the rules are the same, the longer you stay, the more you earn where you have to be right just once until expiry. Your losses will be capped, and risk reward would be in your favour. Time will still be on your side, and even if the market moves just a little in your direction, you get all the results. When you are buying an option, whether it is bearish or bullish, you are always losing money through theta decay even if the market is moving in your predicted direction. When you are strategising to capture points on the same direction, time and intrinsic are both on your side, and you don't lose money with every passing second, instead you gain it. Strategising in options is almost necessary, because with a buy, if you don't get an exit as soon as you enter, you are stuck in there forever, whereas in a sell or a strategy, there is no predefined point of entry or exit, as long as the market is favourable to you, it is your choice how long you want to ride it, and a bearish spread or a bullish spread does wonders especially in changing trends.

Ratio Back Spread

A combination that reduces or eliminates your loss in a trade even when you are wrong

Ratio back spread is a strategy where you sell a particular option, and buy two options near it, depending on whether you are bullish or bearish on the market.

In this strategy, you need to be right or wrong, you cannot be not right, but you can be wrong, which means you need the market to move. Your loss in this strategy is when the market does not move. If you are bullish, and the market goes bearish, you earn something, but if you are right, you earn infinitely and vice versa. Think of it as just buying an option without losing money if you are wrong.

Ratio back spread can be used for both bullish and bearish trade. Let us take a look how.

Bullish Call Ratio Back Spread

Call Ratio Back Spread is a strategy where you gain infinitely, but lose just a fraction. Think of it as a buying a call, but where your money does not get wiped off if you are wrong. In this strategy, you sell one call option at the current strike price, and then buy two call options further ahead. Now, the trick here is to try and sell the call option at double or more than double of what you are buying. In that case, you earn a fixed amount even if the market is bearish, but if the market becomes bullish, your earnings are exponential. This acts as simple as buying a call option, but your losses are capped even if you are wrong. The only problem with this strategy is that you lose money if the market does not move. You win if it bearish, you win if it bullish, but if the market does not move, you lose your premium on sell as well as buy. If you are confident that the market is going to be bullish by the time your contract expires, this is an extraordinary strategy to gain without the risk of theta decay or incurring heavy losses, but you need the movement.

Bearish Put Ratio Back Spread

Put Ratio Back Spread works just like call ratio, but here you need to play around with put options and they work in a bearish trade. Again, in this strategy, you need to sell a put option at the current strike price, and buy two put options a few strike prices below. You need to keep the double or more ratio intact, to earn on both the sides. Here, even if the market goes bullish, triggers short covering, sets new all time highs, you will still get a guaranteed return, but if the market goes bearish as you predicted, you are bound to earn endlessly. With every point in your direction, you keep earning more. When buying put options, you have to worry about theta decay, and you might exit your positions even if you predict a further move, but are not sure as to when it will come, but in this strategy, you have no theta loss, and with every point in your direction, you keep earning, no matter when it happens. You only need it to move.

Long Calendar

A combination of buying and
selling options across expiries

In a long calendar strategy, you buy and sell call or put options across different expiries to gain the premium on your options depending on whether you are bullish, bearish or neutral on the market.

In this strategy, you have to predict an approximate range of the market i.e. where will the market be at the time of the expiry of your contract. You get a wide range that covers you even if you are wrong, but in this strategy, you cannot be extremely right.

Long Calendar strategies are used for bullish, bearish and neutral markets. Let us take a look how.

Bullish Long Calendar with Calls

In Long Calendar with Calls, you sell a call option a few strike prices above the current strike price for the current expiry, or the expiry you are targeting, and you buy the same strike price for the end of the month if you are targeting the first or second week, but if you are in the end of the month, you buy the option for the next month's expiry. All you have to do is to maintain a gap of a few weeks to a month between your buy and sell contracts. Here, you will earn even if the market does not go in your direction, and just stays there with just a few points against you. You will earn the maximum at the strike price that you have targeted on the day of the expiry. If the market reaches your target, good, but if the market breaches your target even on the bullish side, you are covered for another few strike prices, but after that the market will breach your green range, and you will incur a loss. This strategy works best in a stable environment where you predict a slow gradual bullish movement, and no volatility. You will have a big enough range on the bullish side, but you to exit in that range, otherwise you will incur a loss, but on the plus side, your loss will always be capped, so even if you get stuck with a breakout during your trade, you will earn again if the market enters back in your range.

Bearish Long Calendar with Puts

Just like Long Calendar with Calls, Long Calendar with Puts works for a bearish trade. In this strategy, you need to sell a put option a few strike prices below the current spot price, and buy the same strike price option for the expiry a few weeks away. Here too, you get rewarded even if you are not wrong, and even if you are right. The strike price you are targeting will be the point of maximum return, and you will get a range for being right. As long as the market stays in that range, you earn with every passing moment, but if the market breaches that range, that is when you incur a loss. Your position is hedged, so your loss will be capped, but a loss is a loss. When planning this strategy, think of where you predict the market to be. When the market gets there, you need to start preparing your exit, consider the leftover green range as your backup, where you let the market test half of your leftover range, and as soon as the halfway point is breached, you exit, no matter what you hope for, no matter how confident you are that this is the bottom, you exit. You need to take away what you have, secure it and then you can create fresh positions again, but have your target in mind.

Neutral Long Calendar

In this strategy, you are neither bearish, nor bullish. This works best when you believe that the market is not going to move in either direction. Here, you sell an option at the current strike price, and while maintaining your gap of weeks, you buy the same strike price option for the expiry far away. You can do this with either put options or call options, depending on which is giving you more premium intake. In here too, you will get a wide range to be right, but it will be equally capped on both sides. This works best in a rangebound market where the market does not move in either direction substantially. You get to just sit and enjoy premium intake without any movement in the market. Think of it as a simple version of a straddle or strangle that we will discuss below, but with hedges on either sides. You will earn maximum at the current strike price on expiry, but you need to mark your exit range, on halfway of your green range on both the sides to be secure.

Condor

A combination of multiple buys
and sells to create a range

In a Condor, you predict a range where the market will be, gaining a flat profit at any point in that range with protection on both sides.

You buy and sell an option on the lower side as well as the upper side to gain the premiums from both your bullish and bearish moves in a single trade with equal profit at any point, and with the added space to exit in the green.

A Condor can be bullish, bearish or neutral depending on where you expect the market to be. But, in this case, if you are wrong, you lose. Your loss will be hedged, but there is no scope of being wrong. Let us take a look at this strategy under various circumstances.

Bullish Condor

In a Bullish Condor, you buy a call a few strike prices above the spot, and then sell a call option almost equal to the number of strike prices you bought. For example, if the market is at hundred, and you bought the call option for the strike price of hundred and ten, you sell the call options of hundred and twenty. Then you sell another call option above at double the strike prices you used before, and sell another call option with the same gap. Continuing the previous example, you sell a call option at hundred and forty, and buy another one at hundred and fifty. Now, in this case, hundred and twenty to hundred and forty will be your most profitable range, where you will get equal profit at any time. After that, you will still be profitable for another few points on both sides, but with a declining profit. This is the range where you exit, this will be your backup green range. Now, while we have taken up the example of market's spot price at hundred, if the index you are trading in is in thousands, your range will be much wider, and you can always increase the gap between your upper range and lower range, but that will be inversely related to your profit. The more the gap, the lesser the profit, and vice versa. But, in all circumstances, your position will be hedged, and you will know the maximum loss under any circumstance.

Bearish Condor

A Bearish Condor is similar to the bullish condor, but it captures a negative range. If you have a bearish range in mind that the market will be at on the date of expiry, this is a great move that maximises your profit. Here, you use put options for your trade, and you buy a put option for a few strikes below, and sell another one maintaining the gap below. Then you sell another put option at the start of your bottom range, and buy with the same gap. Continuing the example of the bullish condor range, when the index is at hundred points, you buy a put option at eighty, and then sell a put option at sixty for your upper range. Then, for your lower range, you sell a put option of forty, and buy one of twenty. Now, your maximum profit range will become forty to sixty, and on both sides you will get a few points to exit with decreasing profits, but profitable nonetheless. In this strategy, if the market never takes up your direction until expiry, you are bound to lose. But, if it does, even momentarily, you will always get a chance to exit in your green range.

Neutral Condor

In a Neutral Condor, you get your maximum profit at the current spot price, and a few points on both sides, with decreasing profit to exit on both the sides with the combination of call and put options. This works well in a non-volatile stable market. Continuing the same example, if the index is at hundred, you sell a put option of eighty, and buy a put option of sixty to create your lower end. Now, on the upper end, you sell a call option of one twenty, and buy a call option of forty. Now, your maximum profitable range will eighty to one twenty with decreasing profits to exit on both sides. If the market breaches the range on either side, you incur a loss, but that loss will be capped. You can increase or decrease the range as per your requirements, but the smaller the range, the higher the profit. And, as always, time is on your side. If the market goes against you momentarily, your neutral condor becomes a bullish condor or a bearish condor, from where the market is right now, and if you have time till expiry, and you were right about your decision, the market might come back in your range, giving you your exit with a better gain. In this case, even if the market does not move at all, you gain, but if it moves too much, you lose.

Butterfly

A combination of multiple buys
and sells to create a minimal loss
range

A Butterfly strategy is similar to condor, but the losses here are minimal if you are wrong, and the profit has a peak point.

In this strategy, your profit is triangular i.e. it has a point where it is maximum, and it is decreasing on both sides, but if you are wrong, the loss is fairly less compared to a condor.

Again, the longer you stay in the trade, the higher the rewards. It can be used for bullish, bearish and neutral strategies with a good enough range. Let us take a look at them.

Bullish Butterfly

In a Bullish Butterfly, you buy a call option a few strikes above your spot price, sell two more calls with equal distance above your buy and then buy one more call above your sell with equal distance. Considering the hundred index example, if the index is at hundred, you buy a call at one hundred and twenty, sell two calls at one hundred and forty, and then buy another call option at one hundred and sixty. Your peak profit will be at your sell level, at one hundred and forty. Now, you will be getting a fairly smaller range of being right, in comparison to condor or other similar strategies. It works best when the market is at a round number, a psychological level, and the market is expected to hover around it in the short term. But, the advantage of this strategy is that, if you see trouble i.e. the market is trying to exit your range, you can exit your trade with just a little profit, and if you are wrong, the losses are really minimal in comparison to your potential profit.

Bearish Butterfly

A Bearish Butterfly is used to find that profitable range in a bearish trade. In this strategy, with the hundred index example, you buy a put option at eighty, sell two put options at sixty, and then buy another put option at forty. Here, your maximum profit will be at sixty, again with minimal losses in case of a breach of range. This strategy is used when the market is just above the psychological level, and the market goes upwards multiple times, but comes back for support. Take a look at open interest, and if the data is still respecting that support and has enough resistance, this strategy has a very high risk reward ratio. This strategy can also be used for an upcoming expiry, because if you are wrong, you lose really less, but gain a lot. The profit will be capped at one point, and in signs of trouble, it is fairly easy to exit while taking a small profit with you. The longer you stay in the trade, the more time will reward you. With a combination of intrinsic and time, this strategy is one of the most favourite strategies of all time.

Neutral Butterfly

A Neutral Butterfly is again a low risk strategy that works best when the market is stuck at a level, and is not looking to break it in the short run. In this strategy, a combination of calls and puts will be used to create a profitable range. Here, you buy a put option a few strikes below your spot price, and sell the put option of the current spot price. Then, you sell a call option of the current spot price, and then buy the call option with the equal distance as your puts a few strikes above your spot price. So, if the index is at hundred, you sell both the call option and the put option for the current spot price at hundred, and then buy a put option at eighty and a call option at one hundred and twenty. Your maximum profit will be at one hundred while giving you a low risk range to get the maximum out of your trade. The longer the market stays in your range, the higher the profit, and if the market even breaches your range, and is about to come back to that psychological level you have predicted for the market, you earn even more. It works best for short term expiries, where the open interest is already supporting your conclusion.

Directional Range

A combination of buys and sells
with unlimited gains and
cushioned unlimited losses

A Directional Range strategy is used when you are confident of the market's moment, and are willing to ride that trend for the long run.

In a directional strategy, you get to be wrong for a few strikes, and the market will reward you even then. But, if you are completely wrong, there is no one that can save you. On the other hand, if you are right, your reward is exponential without any worry of theta decay, because time is irrelevant here.

Directional Range can be used for bullish and bearish trends, let us see how.

Bullish Range Forward

In a Bullish Range Forward, you use a combination of buying calls and selling puts to achieve the desired result. You buy a call option a few strikes above the current strike price and sell a put option with the same distance on the upside. Continuing with the index of hundred, you buy a call option of one hundred and twenty, and sell a put option of eighty. Now, depending on when you enter the trade, your downside can be mildly negative or positive till the level of eighty. Even if you are somewhat wrong, you still earn something and if you are right, you earn exponentially on the upside with every point the market moves without the worry of theta decay because that is nullified. The only problem with this trade is that if you are completely wrong i.e. the market takes a bearish trend, your liability is infinite. You will be protected till eighty in the above example, but with every point beyond that you start losing with every point in the market. This strategy works best in neutral to bullish trend market with no risk of bearishness. Although this strategy is not recommended, the gains are exponential if you are right, but if you are wrong, you can wipe off your complete capital easily.

Bearish Range Backward

In Bearish Range Backward, you earn with every point the market falls. Here, you sell a call option a few strikes below the current spot price, and in turn, you buy a put option with the same distance strikes on the upside. So, if the market is at hundred, you sell the call option of eighty and in turn, you buy the put option of one hundred and twenty. Here too, you get a cushion to be wrong and are rewarded depending upon when you enter the trade, and get highly rewarded with every point in your direction. The only problem is that if the market takes a bullish direction instead, there is nothing that can save you. You have no hedge to survive it. While the gains are exponential on the bearish side, the fall easily wipes off your capital. Only enter this trade if you are sure that you cannot be wrong even momentarily, because that is all it takes to lose everything, otherwise adapt the next strategy for similar results.

Hedged Directional Range

A variation of directional range
with a proper hedge in place

In the Directional Range, while your gains were infinite, your losses were infinite too. This variation of Directional Range hedges your position to cap your downside and lets you stay in the trade even if you are blatantly wrong for the moment, with scope of being right until expiry.

Hedged Directional Range adds a hedge to your sell by buying an option below or above what you have sold, which protects you from unlimited losses, theta decay and keeps your profit intact.

Hedged Directional Range can be used for bullish as well as bearish trades. Let us see how.

Bullish Hedged Range Forward

In a Bullish Hedged Range Forward, you lose your cushion to minimal losses, and after that instead of unlimited losses, you cap your losses. In this strategy, you still buy a call option above the current spot price, and sell a put option with equal gap on the downside, but you add buying a put option a few strikes below your put option sell. So, if the index is at hundred, you buy a call option of one hundred and twenty, sell a put option of eighty and buy a put option of seventy. The further you buy, the more the possibility of loss, and more the possibility of profit. You go in this trade keeping in mind that this put option will become zero, but just in case things turn around, there is a war, there is an attack, a political assassination anywhere in the world, you are protected. While it will eat at your profits, this is your last defence and if you were right, you will be rewarded as the market turns bullish.

Bearish Hedged Range Backward

A Bearish Hedged Range Backward works just like a Bullish Hedged Range Forward, but for your bearish trade. In this strategy, you sell a call option a few strikes above your current spot price, buy a put option keeping the same gap on the downside, and then buy another call option a few strikes above your call option sell. So, if the index is at hundred, you sell a call option of one hundred and twenty, buy a put option of eighty and then, buy another call option of one hundred and thirty. This lets you earn exponentially in your bearish trend, all the while protecting you on the upside. Your cushion without hedge will become mildly negative, but your infinite loss beyond that will become just a little more negative. But, if you are right, this hedge becomes irrelevant and the gain is extremely high. You have to decide whether you want to earn patiently or do you want to wipe off your capital, just in case you are wrong.

Synthetic Future

A combination of buys and sells
used for immediate profit

A Synthetic Future strategy replicates the futures with options without bearing the premium to spot i.e. you earn with every point in your direction without the worry of theta decay, and the loss and profit is exponential. This strategy is fairly popular among those looking to trade in futures, but replicating the same result with options due to lower margin requirements.

In this strategy, the possibility of gain and loss is infinite, and it is used in both bullish and bearish strategies, to capture every point the market moves without worrying about theta decay. Let us take a look how.

Bullish Long Synthetic Future

A Bullish Long Synthetic Future is a combination of buying a call option and selling a put option. In the example of the hundred index, you buy the call option for hundred and sell the put option for hundred as well. For every point the market gains, you gain accordingly without the worry of theta decay. Even if the market does not move till expiry, and moves even one point in your favour, you earn something. This strategy works extremely well after a correction when the market is regaining its highs. The problem with this strategy is that if you are wrong, there is nothing to protect you. You can easily lose all your capital because with every point the market moves against you, you lose accordingly. So, this strategy should only be adapted if you are sure beyond any doubt of the market's direction, because if you are wrong, this is the easiest way to wipe off your capital.

Bearish Short Synthetic Future

A Bearish Short Synthetic Future works opposite to the bullish long synthetic future where with every point the market falls, you gain and every point the market rises, you lose. In this strategy, you buy a put option and sell a call option for the current spot price. In the example of the hundred index, you buy a put option at hundred and sell a call option at hundred as well. Synthetic Future works just like Futures, but with lesser premium and no theta decay. This strategy works best when there is a negative news and the market is reacting accordingly. It could be a war on the horizon, or political tensions, or even elections. If the market is going to become cautious due to an event, this strategy rewards you exponentially, but if the market reacts the other way, and turns bullish, you are going to lose with every point the market rises with nothing to protect you. If you want to play it safe and replicate the results, the next strategy should work better for you.

Hedged Synthetic Future

A combination of buying snd selling put to hedge your synthetic future

A Hedged Synthetic Future replicates the results of the Synthetic Future strategy, but while protecting you on the downside if you are wrong.

Here, you buy the option you are buying, but with your sell, you add another buy on the same side. If you are right while taking the trade, you will be obviously protected, but in case you are wrong, your liability is not unlimited, but rather capped. If you are right, you will be rewarded, but if you are wrong, would you want to lose it all.

A Hedged Synthetic Future is used for both Bullish and Bearish trades, let us see how.

Bullish Hedged Synthetic Future

A Bullish Hedged Synthetic Future is a combination of buying a call option at the current spot price, selling a put option at the current spot price, and buying another put option just below your sell, depending on your risk appetite. In the example of the hundred index, you buy a call option at hundred, sell a put option at hundred and buy another put option at ninety. You have to understand that if you are right, your put option is net loss, but if you are right and the market moves in your direction more than your put premium loss, the rewards are exponential and theta decay is negligible. If you enter the trade and exit immediately with your gain, your theta impact is zero, but if you stay in the trade for the long run, you need some movement on the bullish side to become profitable by overcoming your put buy. This works marvellously after a correction, and even if the market corrects more for a few more days, you have no worry to exit as your loss is capped. You can wait and enjoy the ride for when the market picks up momentum and turns bullish.

Bearish Hedged Synthetic Future

A Bearish Hedged Synthetic Future works just like you Bullish Hedged Synthetic Future, but it protects you on the upside. In this strategy, you buy a put option at the current spot price, sell a call option at the current spot price, and buy a call option just above it. In the example of the hundred index, you buy a put option at hundred, you sell a call option at hundred and then buy a call option at hundred and twenty. Now, with every point the market falls, you start earning. This works best when the market is supposed to fall with a news on the horizon. It might not fall today, it might not fall tomorrow, but it will fall. For example, in the pandemic, the markets held up in the beginning, but the fall was imminent. Your position is hedged until the market falls, and you can comfortably wait for it. The market might even jump for a dead cat bounce, but you will not panic as your maximum loss is capped, and you do not have to worry about theta decay, because if you are right, time becomes irrelevant after the first move.

Naked Option Sell

A strategy to sell an option for a
directional or neutral move

Naked Option Sell works as in reverse to option buy, that is you sell an option of the strike where you think the market will not breach on either side.

While buying an option, theta decay eats you up every day, every minute, every second, but with an option sell, time rewards you every day, every minute, every second. In this strategy, if planned well, both intrinsic and time value can work together to reward you.

Naked Option sell is used for bullish as well as bearish trades. Let us see how.

Bullish Naked Put Sell

In a Bullish Naked Put Sell, you simply sell a put option and enjoy the theta decay as well as the intrinsic value. In the example of hundred index, you sell the put option for hundred or eighty or fifty, whatever you are comfortable that the market will not breach. With every passing moment that the market does not become bearish, you earn. Even if the market does not move at all, you earn. If the market becomes bullish, you earn rapidly. Your profit will be capped, but it is usually a good return. If the market is not moving, time makes you earn with decay. If the market is bullish, time and intrinsic both make you earn together. But, even if the market becomes bearish for just a few points, and you had a good premium before you entered the trade, you are bound to earn. If the market reaches your selling strike price, but does not breach it, you still earn hundred percent on expiry. The only problem with this trade is that if the market becomes bearish, and breaches your strike price, you start losing with every point against you and there is no cap to your loss. The more the market falls, the more you lose. This strategy must be planned with extreme caution, but it has its rewards for the risk taken.

Bearish Naked Call Sell

A Bearish Naked Call Sell is selling a call option at the strike price you predict for the market to not breach on the upside. In the example of the hundred index, you can sell a call option for hundred, one hundred and twenty, one hundred and forty, whatever you are comfortable with and positive that the market will not breach. Again, in this case, you earn even if the market does not move at all, and also if the market is bearish. All you have to do is not be wrong, and the market will reward you with time and intrinsic in your favour. But, in case you are wrong and the market turns bullish, you have nothing to protect you and your losses are infinite. The risk reward ratio is good, that is why it is the most common strategy used by traders, but in case you are not looking for unlimited risk, the next strategy with a hedge should work better for you. Naked selling is not recommended, but it has its rewards and works wonders for those who have a risk appetite.

Hedged Option Sell

A combination of buys and sells
to hedge your naked selling

In a Naked option sell, you sold the put or call options with great rewards, but unlimited liability. In this strategy, you sell the same options, but you buy something to protect you against unlimited liability.

In this strategy, you sell your options like before, but you buy the same side option at a lower or higher strike price as insurance. The gap can be really close or really far depending on your risk appetite, but your losses will always be capped, no matter the change in the dynamics.

A Hedged Option Sell is used for both Bullish and Bearish trades, and is highly recommended. Let us see how.

Bullish Hedged Put Sell

In a Bullish Hedged Sell, you sell a put option and then buy another put option for the same expiry. In the example of the hundred index, you can sell a put option for hundred, eighty, one hundred and twenty, wherever you predict the market to be above, and buy another put option at your choice below your sell, as much as you are willing to risk in case you are wrong. You should only sell the put option above the spot price after a correction or in a highly bullish trend, because you need the market to breach that strike price for you to become profitable. The gains are better when you sell a higher strike price, but you will be dependant more on intrinsic, rather than time value. Time will only play in your team if the market breaches your sell. Your hedge put option buy can have a lot of gap or minimal gap depending on what you are intending to earn from this trade, and what you are willing to risk. As always, the longer you stay in the trade, the higher the reward. But, if the market becomes highly bullish, even intrinsic can give you your maximum reward.

Bearish Hedged Call Sell

In a Bearish Hedged Sell, you are predicting the market to not breach a certain strike price on the upside. In this strategy, you sell a call option, and buy another call option below it with the gap depending on your risk reward. In the example of the hundred index, you can sell the call option for hundred, hundred and twenty, or even eighty while buying a call option below your sell. You should only sell a call option in the money i.e. below the spot price if you are sure of a bearish moment coming soon, otherwise you should only sell at the money or out of the money, which provides you a bit of security and rewards you even if the market does not turn bearish or even move at all. Your hedge can have the gap that you are willing to risk. The more the gap, the more the reward, the higher the risk. But, in any circumstance, even if you are blatantly wrong, your loss will always be capped. Before entering the trade, you will be aware of the maximum you can earn or the maximum you can lose. Hedged option selling is the most commonly used strategy in trading because it is the perfect balance of rewards, theta decay and risk management.

Batman

A combination of buys and sell
to create a batman pattern of
profit

The Batman strategy is a combination of multiple buys and sells with maximum profit on the outer range and a good enough profit in the huge middle range to depict the mask of batman in your profits.

In this strategy, you sell four lots and buy two lots, which gives you substantial profit, but is prone to unlimited liability if the market becomes directional and breaks your range.

The Batman strategy is used in neutral trades with a huge profitable range. Let us see how.

Neutral
Batman

The Batman strategy involves buying a call option and a put option at the current spot price, and selling two call options just above your call buy and then selling two put options just below your put buy. In the example of the hundred index, you buy a call option at hundred, you buy a put option at hundred, and sell two call options at one hundred and ten, and then sell two put options at ninety. This gives you an extremely profitable wide range for the market to stay in with extraordinary profits, and even more profits at the outer range i.e. the batman's ear. The only downside to this strategy is that if the market breaches your batman's mask range, the downside on either side is unlimited as you have an extra call and put sell in your trade which is not hedged. If you want to adapt this strategy, but want to play it a little safe, the next strategy should be perfect for you.

Hedged Batman

A combination of multiple buys and sells to hedge your Batman strategy

A Hedged Batman strategy involves more or less the same principles, but adding an extra call and put buy to your basket that protects you on both the sides. The mask remains intact i.e. your profit will be maximised on the outer range, and you will get a flat profit in the middle range, but it cuts down your non hedged profit substantially.

In this strategy, you sell four lots and buy four lots, but at different strike prices to maintain your batman strategy along with giving you insurance on both the sides. Let us take a look how.

Neutral Hedged Batman

A Hedged Batman Strategy involves buying the call option and the put option at the current spot price, and then selling two call options just above the your call buy and selling two put options just below your put buy. After that, to hedge your positions, you also buy a call option a few strikes above your call buy, and a put option few strikes below your put buy. In the example of hundred index, you buy a call option at hundred, a put option at hundred, and then you sell two call options at one hundred and twenty, two put options at eight and finally to hedge your positions, you buy one call option at one hundred and fifty, and one put option at fifty. This gives you a wide enough profitable range, but in comparison to batman, the profits are much lesser. It will be your choice whether you want limited profits with negligible losses or do you want higher profits, with possibility of unlimited losses. Your decision will depend a lot on the market trend, but you should always try and hedge your positions whenever possible.

Double Plateau

A combination of put and sells to protect you on the bullish as well as bearish trade

A Double Plateau strategy is basically a balanced condor on the bullish as well as bearish side. For this strategy to work, you need the market to move in either direction, but it needs to move. Your losses will be capped if it does not, but if it does you will be well rewarded.

In this strategy, you use a combination of four buys and sells to achieve your desired ranges on the bullish as well as bearish side. It is used for a neutral trade where you are not sure as to the direction the market will take, but are positive of a move in either direction. Let us see how we can use this strategy.

Neutral
Double
Plateau

A Neutral Double Plateau uses a combination of buying a call option just above the current spot price, selling a call option of a higher strike from the spot price, selling another call option a bit higher from your previous sell and then finally buying another call option with the equal gap from your sell. Then, on the downside, you sell buy a put option much lower than your spot price, and sell a put option near to your buy, then you sell another put option near your spot price, and finally buy another put option much lower than your first put option buy. To simplify it in the hundred index example chronologically, you buy a call option at one hundred and ten, sell a call option at one hundred and thirty, sell another call option at one hundred and fifty, and buy one call option at one hundred and eighty. Similarly on the downside, you buy a put option at fifty, sell a put option at thirty, sell another put option at twenty, and buy another option at ten. Basically you are putting both the bullish condor and the bearish condor in a single range to get rewarded wherever the market goes by the time of expiry. All you need is for the market to be in either of the ranges by expiry. Again, the longer you stay, the better the gain and you can exit anytime you think the market is about to breach either of the range. All the while, your losses will be capped at a minimal loss with theta decay and intrinsic value playing for you on both the bearish and bullish sides.

Hero Zero

A combination of buys on the
day of the expiry to eliminate
the theta decay and gain

A Hero Zero strategy is used on expiry day to buy options for both sides and gain with movement in either direction without worrying about theta decay.

In a Hero Zero strategy, you do not sell any option, but just buy the options on both sides and expect the market to move more than the premium on one side. It is used for a directional trade with minimal movement in the index on the day of the expiry.

Let us see how to use Hero Zero optimally.

Neutral Hero Zero

A Hero Zero strategy is used when you are uncertain of the market's direction even if the movement is minimal and you want to earn on either side. In this strategy, you buy both the call and put option at the current spot price on the day of the expiry, just hours before closing. In the example of hundred index, you buy both the call option and the put option at hundred, the trick is to total the call and put side premium, and the premium must be less than or equal to the difference of the next strike price.

If the next strike price is at one hundred and ten or ninety, the total of the premium of the call and the put side must be less than or equal to ten. With this strategy, your losses are negligible and with just a little moment of even one strike price, you break even or even be profitable depending on the time of the moment, and if the market takes either direction, your gains are exponential. The only loss you suffer is if the market does not move at all, but even then the losses are minimal.

Strip Strap

A combination of buys with gains
on either side

A Strip Strap strategy is used when the market has a news on the horizon and can take either direction, but whichever way it goes, it moves with momentum in that direction.

In Strip and Strap, you buy the call or put options with one double depending on the direction you are predicting for the market. If the market moves in that direction, you earn exponentially, but even if it does not, you still earn if the movement is big.

Strip Strap strategy is used for bullish as well as bearish trades. Let us see how.

Bullish Strap

In a Bullish Strap strategy, you buy two call options and one put option at the current spot price. In the example of the hundred index, you buy two call options at hundred and one put option at hundred. If the market becomes bullish, you earn almost double, but even if the market takes a bearish trend, the put becomes double to your call buys. When you have two calls, you will easily overcome the cost of buying a put option with movement in your favour, but if the trend becomes bearish, you need more movement on the side you are wrong for it to cover the cost of your call options and then give you gain. This strategy is really useful during times of huge movement based on news in either direction like election results. The downside to this strategy is that if the market does not move at all in either direction, you lose your call premiums as well as put premium to theta decay. Time is not your friend in this strategy. You need the market to move as soon as possible.

Bearish Strip

A Bearish Strip is opposite to a bullish strap. Here, you buy two put options and one call option at the current spot price favouring a fall in the market rather than a rise. In the example of hundred index, you buy two put options at hundred and one call option at hundred. If the market becomes bearish, you earn faster and more, but even if it takes a bullish trend, you still earn after the cost of your put options is exceeded. All you need is a trend in either direction. Time is your biggest enemy here as the losses are great if there is no movement in the market. Adapt this strategy only in times of uncertainties, corrections and event based days. Your goal is to not ride this strategy till expiry, but get in and get out a soon as the event is done with your profits.

Mix Match

A Mix Match strategy has no
particular set of rules but rather
mixes multiple strategies

A Mix Match strategy involves incorporating multiple strategies into one trade to amplify your profitable range or to maximise your profits. You can use a hedged synthetic future with a condor or hedged batman with an option sell depending on where you are predicting the market to be and how much do you intend to gain from that trade. If you somewhat believe in a trade you already are, but the market shows some risk of breaching your range, you can add another trade where your profits of the range remain secure if the market ends in that range, but even if it breaches your range, another trade comes in to protect you and continue your gains. While adding multiple strategies in a single trade, you can reduce your profit and concentrate it on a single strike or increase your range. In an alternate case, if you are sure of your trade, but want a bigger range, you can add an enveloping trade where your maximum profit is where you predict it to be, but there is some profit on the outer range too. It can be any combination depending upon the market direction and your goal while entering the trade, or the goal can simply be an adjustment to your positions. Backtest the combination before placing an order to know your breakeven points, your point of maximum profit and the estimated profit at various strike prices.

Deep ITMs

A strategy to sell Deep In The Money options

Deep In the Money options are calls or puts that are away from the spot price, but the market has a potential to attain them. If you are positive about the market attaining that strike price until expiry, you need to sell them and buy an At The Money call or put option to hedge your position. Now, if the market attains that strike price, your gains are high, but even if the market does not attain that, but ends near it, you will still be in a good profit. Moreover, if you are wrong, these calls already have very less premium and your loss is capped very low. Deep ITM option selling is used when the market is in a trend or after a correction when the market is going to retrace to previous highs. For selling deep ITM options, you need to have ample amount of time before expiry, so that even if the market is not yet ready to achieve your predicted strike price, there is still potential for the market to attain it in the time left until expiry. The longer the market takes to get there, the better will be your profit after the market attaining it.

Definite OTMs

Selling Deep Out Of The Money options

This strategy works only a day before the expiry or on the day of the expiry to get the best results with risk management. In this strategy, you sell deep out of the money options which there is no possibility for the market to attain. This does not need to your primary trade, but just some extra money on the day of expiry on the idle money you have in your trading account. If on the date of the expiry, you get an opportunity to sell a call option thousands of points away, which the market has no possibility to attain without breaking the upper circuit, the premium on that call is free money for you. You sell the call option and by the end of the day, you have that premium in your bank account with almost zero risk. The reward might not be high, but considering zero risk on your idle money with guaranteed profit in your account by the end of the day is a good deal. Never use this strategy for your put options because while the strike of your call option is almost impossible, a war in another country is a possibility which drops the market immediately. You should not risk betting against the fall with negligible reward. Always use this strategy for call option selling on the day of the expiry, and you are next to guaranteed to earn something with zero risk. It is literally free money, why not grab it. These positions cannot be hedged, otherwise there will be almost negligible reward, so while this strategy is ninety nine percent safe, at the first sign of trouble, if you ever encounter such a situation, exit your positions without a second thought, since the risk is not worth the rewards. But, almost always you will be thousands of points away from your risk zone.

Epilogue

The market is not perfect, the game is not perfect, but the market does not care who are you and what your trade is. There is nobody out to get you. It is just you against yourself. There is money going all around, do you the discipline and the capability to grab it ? The market will do what it intends to do, the question is are you going against the flow, or with the flow, and most of all how right are you in predicting the flow. If you pair proper risk management with proper strategies, you are almost sure to win. You might lose once or twice, but almost always at the end, you will be in the green, and at the end, it is all about the money.

The Game of
Futures and
Options

Playing the Game of Futures & Options

Playing the Game of Futures & Options

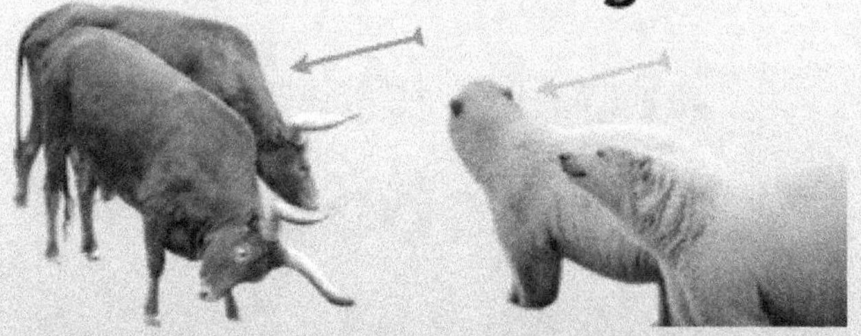

Your rulebook to Win

Bill Lucre

Stock Market
Rulebook

Playing the Game of the Stock Market

Bill Lucre